Stress Management For Kids

Melinda Perry

Copyright © 2020 Melinda Perry

All rights reserved. No part of this publication may be reproduced, distributed, or transmitted in any form or by any means, including photocopying, recording, or other electronic or mechanical methods, without the prior written permission of the publisher, except in the case of brief quotations embodied in critical reviews and specific other non-commercial uses permitted by copyright law.

ISBN: 978-1-63750-258-7

Table of Contents

STRESS MANAGEMENT FOR KIDS 1

INTRODUCTION 5

CHAPTER 1 7
    REALIZING STRESS IN KIDS 7

CHAPTER 2 9
    FACTORS BEHIND TENSION 9

CHAPTER 3 13
    TENSION SYMPTOMS 13

CHAPTER 4 16
    EFFECTS OF STRESS 16

CHAPTER 5 19
    STRESS ADMINISTRATION TIPS 19

CHAPTER 6 24
    MANAGING SCHOOL STRESS 24

CHAPTER 7 29
    HELPING KIDS REDUCE STRESS 29

CHAPTER 8 32
    STRESS RELIEVER ONLINE GAMES 32

CHAPTER 9 36
    STRESS RELIEVING EXERCISES 36

CHAPTER 10 39
    WHAT MAKES CHILDREN ANXIOUS TODAY? 39
        Indicators of Stress in Kids 39
        What Parents Can Carry out About Kid Stress 41
        How to handle Anxiety in Children 43

Maintain Your Son or Daughter's Health 45

CHAPTER 11 ....**48**

PREVENTING VACATION ANXIETY AND STRESS IN CHILDREN. 48

CHAPTER 12 ....**53**

HANDLING ANXIETY AND STRESS IN KIDS 53
   Signs of Stress in Kids 53
   Common Factors behind Child Years Stress 55

CHAPTER 13 ....**62**

STRESS MANAGEMENT IDEAS 62
   Breathing Approaches for Stress Relief 64
   Breathing Focus 65
INTENSIFYING MUSCLE MASS RELAXATION 67
   Modified Lion's Breath 68
   Five Methods For A Sensible Existence 70
   Great things about Routine workouts 71
   Manage Stress in healthful ways 73
   Much Healthier Methods to Control Stress: 75
   Harmful ways to cope with stress: 76
   Dangerous Effects of ongoing Stress: 76

Introduction

This book will work you through steps to follow to effectively manage your stress and also the stress in your children the natural way.

People who figure out how to deal with stress and business live a happier, healthier life, because a sound body is a formidable tool to fight stress.

This book also gives information about how to realize tension in kids, the symptoms, stress reliever games that would help both kids and adults, stress relieving exercises, what makes children anxious and what parents are expected to do, and how positive thinking can assist you in healing and ultimately move forward in life. You would find several ways to manage stress, such as controlling your thoughts, managing your emotions, eating healthy, exercise as a routine and more.

As you read further on what to do to help your children manage stress effectively, and also to manage your stress, You would be glad you did because this book explains basic mechanisms of stress and relaxation and offers research-based guidance for improving treatment outcomes.

Chapter 1

Realizing Stress in Kids

Through the bogeyman for small kids to the bogies of SATs and the last exams intended for the college-bound, it has been carefully observed that stress affects kids of most ages; the very first thing a mother or father can do to help the youngster manage tension and anxiety is to create a substantial family device, which includes the constant conversation with the kids so as to get acquainted with their psychological state of being tense.

Kids especially, with under-developed communications abilities, may extremely screen anxiety in a different way than a grown-up will. Often time, kids' stress is usually internalized & most apparently in a physical perceived sensation such as regular flu-like symptoms, which include headache, stomachache, and even nausea.

Children below anxiety might regress to habits like bedwetting, clinginess, and regular crying; these symptoms might be intense, as an ordinarily energetic child turns, into either listless or hyper-active, a generally docile kid has suits of anger or a kid that "functions out" becomes bright and reflective.

Some indications of tension in children are easily confused with children's mental disorders. For example, your child's close friends go through an extreme switch, anxiety, and emotional stress might step in at this point and situations such as that may reveal a child's inability to take care of a demanding circumstance.

Just as much as tension is an integral part of grownups' lives today, so it is, progressively an essential part of kids' lives as well, this means stress administration for kids should be a primary topic parents must comprehend and understand. Child tension and mature stress often come up due to lots of factors that may be entirely resolved by merely studying the actual problem, which may be leading to child tension, after which taking procedure for helping a kid feel better and calmer.

Chapter 2

Factors behind Tension

Tension can be said to have one cause, which is the awareness and response to the circumstances that happen in our lives. Stress could be triggered simply by something as simple as breaking a fingernail. Furthermore, the positive occasions in our lives are often as nerve-racking as harmful types.

For instance, the delivery of a kid could be stressful negatively, and positively. If the baby is a boy or a girl, it doesn't matter; however, it is beautiful, and at that point, our adrenaline moves and beam with satisfaction since our mind fills up with jubilation and overwhelming feelings. Frequent stress comes after, thought to begin to flow through the mind, e.g., *"Will we be considered a great mother or father? Will I give birth to another child? Will I have to wake up every 2 am when the baby is crying?"*

There are two basic types of stress; the first is named **eustress or positive pressure**, while the second is **distress** *or unfavorable anxiety*. Dealing with ***eustress*** is more straightforward than working with pain; the simple truth is that whether positive or negative, tension stresss.

Furthermore, what may be considered a stress reliever to someone may be viewed as a stressor to another; for example, "the divorce may be alleviation for just one party" or "a calamity that results to a job lay-off, which can provide one much needed holiday and at the same time can cause financial catastrophe."

Whatever causes tension or stress is called a *stressor*, usually the type of stress most people are concerned about happen to be "distress"; possibly processive stressor or systemic stressors can trigger this negative tension.

Processive stressors are the ones that generate what is known as the *"fight or flight"* reaction. Whenever we believe there is a severe immediate danger, the pituitary gland instantly noises a security alarm by merely liberating a burst of adrenocorticotropic body hormone (ACTH), which indicates the adrenal glands and then release the *"stress human hormones"* which are *adrenaline and cortisol.*

These human hormones are, in fact, a guard that helps us concentrate on the situation, speed up response times, and briefly increase our physical power and agility while we determine whether to retreat or stand.

A systemic stressor is the bodies' automated physiological reactions to tension, like the lack of equilibrium (dizziness) that you are feeling before you faint or maybe the release of acid solution that turns and churns your stomach throughout a nerve-racking scenario.

The systemic stressor may be released concurrently along with processive stressors and may cause much more stress because they create a more substantial sensation of risk to your wellbeing.

Although the suffering from tension has happened to everyone at one time or another, and study indicates that children who also reside in a burdensome housing environment are at higher risk of being anxious by life's challenges.

Furthermore, some analysis shows that in both processive

and systematic occasions, people find the capability to handle the stress triggered by all those occasions partially hereditary, governed by genes that control the endorphin amounts. (Endorphins will be the human hormones that control the moods and also become an all-natural "pain killer").

Although events might appear stress filled, it's essential to keep in mind that tension is established simply by our reactions to circumstances, as opposed to the occasions themselves.

The truth is, stress can be "all in our mind." Placing life's fluctuations into proper perspective is the main element in dealing with stress, and the consequence is wearing both our health, wellness, and our lives.

Chapter 3

Tension Symptoms

The symptoms of anxiety are our physical, psychological, and behavioral response to life's situations.

- The pounding of our minds as the house team rates the successful point.

- The sensation of disappointment when the other group scores the winning stage.

- The lively hooray whenever we win as well as the angry problem whenever we drop.

Degrees of tension are classified as ***extreme, episodic severe, and persistent.*** Stress symptoms tend to be a sign of the degree of anxiety. Severe anxiety is the short-term kind of pressure we feel, for instance, whenever we stage back again to the curb from the path of the oncoming automobile, or when the house group wins (or manages to lose).

This sort of stress is the most workable. Our center rates

leap, bloodstream stresses raise, pressure headaches might ensue, we all become briefly upset, optimistic, boisterous, or resentful. All of us cry in pleasure, in comfort, in frustration as soon as days go by and continue regarding or business.

Episodic severe stress happens when life's situations obtain the best folks when Murphy's Law appears to be the guideline of your day. One of these is usually is when life situations rotate uncontrollably with one devastation after another - a sickness, the divorce, and lack of work in a short while.

Symptoms like recurring headaches, indigestion, exhaustion, and sleeping disorders are vibrant indicators of episodic desperate stress. We can avoid occasional severe tension by realizing its signs and dealing with difficult circumstances as they take place. Without interest, this degree of stress can result in *chronic anxiety*.

Chronic anxiety/tension is whatever literally would wear one out, grinding one down till our anatomies and minds respond with severe long-term physical or mental disorders. Persistent stress takes place when circumstances become difficult to cope with when there's "no chance out," and we quit trying to conquer adversity.

Regrettably, once tension becomes persistent, long-overlooked symptoms become unseen. Milling tooth, tremors, misunderstandings, forgetfulness, over-eating, and alcoholism are just some of the signs that look like practices that are as durable as the situations that triggered all of them.

Stress indicators can help all of us measure the degree of tension. However, tension symptoms frequently overlap in one level to another. Moreover, many symptoms of stress could be triggered simply by physical disease or mental disorders.

Spotting stress symptoms can help us keep stress and anxiety from snowballing, from severe to persistent, quickens us to get medical help whenever we require it and maintain us from struggling the debilitating Effects of stress.

Chapter 4

Effects of Stress

The consequences of worry can significantly affect one's existence for either better or worse. That extra rush of adrenalin, released during severe stress, provides us with a needed burst open of speed whenever we run away from risk or a supplementary surge of power whenever we opt to stand and battle.

However, whenever we neglect to launch stress by merely dealing with life's situations, this accumulates until we possibly explode or collapse. The results of tension can cause particular disorders in both body and mind. Furthermore, to the raising degrees of the stress human hormones, adrenaline, and corticosterone; an accumulation of tension can cause headaches, digestive problems, eating disorders, sleeping disorders, exhaustion, and lower the level of resistance to other ailments like the common cold and flu.

Whenever we are deluged with a series of stressful

circumstances, our anatomies do not give time for you to change; neither does our thoughts give time to help make the decisions essential to offer with pressure in a wholesome manner.

That is episodic tension. As time passes, unrelieved stress, like occasional tension, can lead to increased heart rate, respiration, and blood circulation pressure, which put unnecessary stress on organs like the heart and lungs.

Ultimately the body offers in the combat; struggling to run away from our complications, we develop more significant complications like cardiovascular disease, high blood pressure, heart stroke, and other health problems.

Psychologically, tension can get so close to burning us away. Long-term pressure becomes persistent stress. The pressure becomes off traffic, hiding in the back of emotions of hopelessness, continuous panic, depressive disorder, and in serious instances, severe mental aberration such as paranoia and delusions. The worst-case result of stress is undoubtedly suicide.

Just like every individual's responses vary, there is no set limit concerning just how much stress every folk can easily endure. Every people appear to be endowed with this own tension "thermometer." When the mercury increases or plummets, we have to possess a well-planned technique to manage anxiety so we can remain healthy as we should. Knowing and utilizing a couple of stress administration tips could make all the difference in the results of concern.

Chapter 5

Stress Administration Tips

Not all anxiety is bad. Stress can bring change, helping us concentrate on the task accessible, and in some instances, even conserve our lives. However, when stress accumulates, it may lead to the opposites- and cause all of us to spin our tires, keep all of us from focusing, and trigger physical damage and even lack of life.

The first suggestion in controlling stress is usually to identify your stressors. The next thing is to put all of them in their place.

The next Stress management hints predicated on a few old and also some new adages will help you perform that!

Take a Breath and Count Number One to Ten - Going for a deep breath provides oxygen to one's body, which is usually very quick and can help you relax. Furthermore, taking an instant to stage back again will help you keep up your composure, which, generally, overtime is definitely what you ought to do rationally through a tense situation.

Focus on "take a breath" and count to 10 (or even more or less mainly till the problem becomes justified!)

Operate and extend - Keep in mind the rest is contrary to stress and anxiety.

Operate and smile - Check it out! You'll feel a lot better!

Take a brief walk – take one glass of drinking water. Take action that changes your concentrate. When you get back to the issue, likely, this won't appear insurmountable.

Available Elimination Using the Wind, *Scarlett O'Hara* says, *"i cannot think about this right now. Easily do, items go crazy. I'll believe this the next day."* Advice!

Stop and Smell the Roses - "Things happen" and sometimes "bad things eventually to good people." If we allow them to, tense occasions can build-up wall structure for all of us, and finally, stop us from taking pleasure in the excellent points in life.

Make an effort - All too often, all of us place the pleasantries of existence on the trunk burner, informing ourselves we all don't "have time" or can't "make time" to them.

However, time can be the thing all of us do own. Even though we can't "make" each day that's much longer than a day, each folk starts the day with precisely that timeframe, have a component of your energy to identify the beautiful items in your daily life.

Sleep Onto It - Every gold coin has two edges. Every concern offers both benefits and drawbacks. List all of them both, in that case, place the list away and have a second look at the next day. Sometimes *"sleeping on"* a predicament changes the minuses to pluses.

Every single cloud includes a metallic coating. In the end, rainfall makes issues develop! Bill Franklin found out good within a bolt of lightning. Discover the nice within your nerve-racking circumstance by listing the harmful surges and identifying what it will require to make sure they are into actual costs!

Know Your Limitations - Understanding yourself as well as your restrictions might be the most basic method of controlling Stress effectively.

Challenges make it at times difficult, making the right decisions stating *yes or no*, yet this decision is another little thing that can be the "straw that breaks the camels back." It is alright to state *"No," "I can't,"* or *"Later."*

Dismiss yourself – Occasionally, situations actually are uncontrollable, and you indeed are *"NOT LIABLE."* Stop blaming yourself.

Be pro-active to find serenity - Those that unsuccessfully use the crutches of medicines or alcoholic beverages to ease Stress often end up in a twelve-step program just like where one of the mainstays is the Tranquility Prayer:

"God grant me personally the Courage to simply accept the things I can not change; The Serenity to improve the things I could; as well as the Knowledge to understand the difference."

If you want help, get help, Even Atlas couldn't carry the weight of the globe on his shoulder blades forever. Whether you will need help from kids or partners in hauling household goods into the home, advice from a friend to resolve a work-related issue, or specialized support to get the factors behind and efficiently manage your stress, obtaining the assistance you will need is alone a significant Stress management suggestion!

Other Suggestions

- Get yourself great nights relax.
- Eat healthily.
- Listen to your preferred music.
- Workout, take part in a sport or take part in any fun activity.
- Map out your time and effort and prioritize.
- Speak with a pal regarding your complications, don't keep it in.
- Get a therapeutic massage.
- Rest.
- Have a warm shower.
- Read a book or watch television.

Chapter 6

Managing School Stress

Understand that old proverb that says *"is the cup half-empty or fifty percent total?"* this adage asks about whether a glass that contains 50 percent water and 50 percent air is half full or half empty, Obviously, regardless of which way you choose to answer, the glass will provide the same amount. Well, this method as regard Stress and peace will not help you control either senior high school or university stress.

Everything you have is undoubtedly a full 12 months before you, but it's instead a year filled with success or a 12 month filled with Stress, depending on your plan.

Among the functions of education, usually, it is to solve problems, and by doing this, prepare yourself for the difficulties of life after college. Learning how to succeed in managing college student stress will undoubtedly bring you quite a distance toward handling Stress over your daily life.

The trick to senior high school and university Stress management is organization.

Take a look at college as you short-term business - You can't work in an office without materials; in the same similitude, ensure that your paper, pencils, pens, files, etc. are readily available. Personal suggestion on how to lessen school stress:

Keep your locker well-organized. It can help you retain promptly and unflustered.

If you want help with a topic, don't hesitate to get a teacher. Educators and professors would be able to offer advice.

Strategize your projects and work out your plan - Routine time designed for research should be strictly adhered to, unless of course, a genuine crisis (open fire, overflow, and famine) gets in the manner. If you want a rest after college, you can rest but take out your time and do research later at night. Remembering that the contrary of stress is usually rest, make sure to timetable both!

Particular Suggestion: Don't allow work build-up to

mess up your weekend. Even if you decide to focus on any part of the Saturday or Sunday, make one of these your "day off." You'll discover that facing the arriving week is a lot easier when you've experienced real-time to refresh!

Figure out How to Prioritize – there are books you'd want to read, and you cannot read all at the same time. You can pick a study time to at least

1. Focus on extended tasks, or

2. Go through a section (or perhaps a few pages) forward.

Choose a friendly Subject Matter - Each time a task permits you to find the subject matter, choose something relating to your passion, not really what you believe will make the educator impressed.

Apart from making assignment more fun and less demanding; good marks result from great work, so do your best to get a good result, and enjoy what you do.

Cramming is a superb method to be filled! It is required to be observed occasionally; nevertheless, you may avoid physical pains and aches (stressors) and innovate blocks by firmly taking a five-minute break after every hour of research.

Be Quick - If you don't have a reasonably thick meticulous study scheme, classroom peanut and educators' intelligence are destined to cause you to be unpleasant. Discover as much as you can in the areas of concentration as regards the examination. Take the benefit of any practice assessments.

Research for the kind of test - Multiple-choice examinations are usually about truth, method, and data mixed. Article assessments typically need you to have knowledge about them and possibly get into fine detail upon a subject or two.

Find out where you're heading – you prepare for the exam before the set time, do not take it for granted.

Make sure everything you need is obtained and organized the night before. Bunch your handbag or briefcase with all you think you will need, which includes a treat, water, calculator, eyeglasses, etc.

Eat before the exam - There might not be enough time or

a chance to consume a meal at that point. Apart from causing you to feel exhausted, a bright belly can also cause you to be stressed and shaky.

Gown for success - Whether you work hot or chilly, the area may be out of your safe zone. Wear a mild coating of clothing following to your skin layer and an appropriate sweater or coat that you could shed in the unneeded event.

Chapter 7

Helping Kids Reduce Stress

Kids mainly learn by examples; they do precisely what they see. The ultimate way to train your son or daughter how to control Stress is to apply the various tools and content articles at *Pressure Management Ideas* to figure out how to successfully manage your stressors. Furthermore, you can form skills and child-oriented Stress management ways to help your children identify and manage their particular stressors.

Consume healthily - A sound body is better in a position to withstand stress-induced disease. Plan regular foods and treat times. Do not allow your son or daughter to miss meals.

Strenuous exercise is an excellent stress reliever - Exactly like adults, kids want time for you to relax. If your children are destined to video gaming, television, or a personal computer, have them on their feet by giving and encouraging the utilization of dynamic playthings like balls, strike handbags, and bikes. If your son or daughter is currently pressured, make a spot of using them. The period spent with your children is a superb vehicle, so you can get them to start the lines of conversation.

Be very clear in establishing rules and constant with self-discipline. Children reside in a "dark and white" world. Blurry recommendations and inconsistencies are even more complicated on their behalf than they may be for all adults.

Mild physical touch is a superb healer - Occasionally a hug will probably be worth more significant than a 1000 words. An additional physical Stress reliever may be considered a mild therapeutic massage of the child's throat and shoulder blades. As if you, your children, can also obtain knotted plan stress!

Learn how to be considered a great listener - Whenever your child desires to discuss his/her complications, don't criticize. Furthermore, it all isn't usually essential to provide advice. Occasionally kids need to chat. Motivate them with open-ended questions like, *"Just what exactly* *occurred?" "How will you experience that?"*

Teach your children that everybody (including you) have faults. An excellent start is usually admitting your errors to your kids with an *"I'm sorry"* or *"My mistake"* when you goof-up. If the problem arrest warrants, use personal types of stressful situations you experienced in your child years. Even though you were not successful in working with your position, you'll train your children that you could study from as well as giggle at your errors.

Finally, train your children worry relieving exercises and help them discover stress-reducing games they will perform to lessen their particular anxiety.

Chapter 8

Stress Reliever Online games

When stress mounts and frustration develops, it's a sure indication of Stress. Playing a stress-reducing game helps you relax, and it's an excellent way to make an impression on anxiety. The secret to stress reliever video games is usually to try out types you can earn easily. What you would like to do is show yourself that you will be successful. Once you get a few "wins" below your belt, regularly, you'll call at your original issue from a fresh perspective.

Video games

From beating a floor hog to batting a rugby ball, you will find loads of flash video games on the internet, and on top of that, the majority are absolving to enjoy! The ultimate way to bunch your anti-stress arsenal can be to execute a simple seek out "Free Adobe flash Video games " or " Display Video games " and bookmark those hateful pounds in your favas. You can even perform the free (or paid) game on your mobile phone or tablet by installing the overall game application to your device.

Off the internet Stress-busting Video games

If you're sitting down all day long with a personal computer, occasionally, the best break is to get right up and leave. Here are some video games that are easy to play and excellent just for assisting you to lessen your stress:

Got a deck of credit cards? Perform an instant video game of solitaire the old-fashioned way! Together with your deck, you may consider investing in a publication of Solitaire video games. Many books are released explicitly for Solitaire players and provide numerous video games and game variants.

- ***Rubik's Dice - Here is a suggestion:*** Anyone may match a single side of the Rubik's dice. Although attempting to solve the complete puzzle could be tense alone, the short while it takes to complement, prevent using one part will help you quickly lessen your Stress.

- ***Slinky*** - Just jumping a slinky backward and

forwards from hand at hand puts your concentrate on the toy and calls for this from your trouble. So jump your slinky, have a couple of deep breaths, and unwind!

- ***Punch tennis balls*** - Ok, they're not a game; however, they can be considered an excellent pressure reliever, and they're sure a much better choice than striking a wall structure or throwing the medial side of the table when stress set in! You'll find cheap impact balls in toy departments, novelty shops, & most buck stores.

- ***Darts*** - Whether you're striking a focus on or focusing on an image, the physical movement of tossing the darts alone can help lessen your stress. Dart golf balls adhere to a Velcro table. They will not harm you or your neighbour -- if you miss!

- ***Crossword Questions*** - Many crossword puzzle books likewise incorporate word-find video games, mazes, and various other pencil questions. Buy several which have questions that range between easy to hard and deal with them regarding your feeling as well as your stress level!

Chapter 9

Stress Relieving Exercises

Although you might not think about exercise simply because it is stress alleviating (if you have ever strolled a treadmill machine for a pressure test), a sound body is a formidable tool to fight stress.

A complete exercise program can't end up being completed at the table, yet several easy exercises can be done to relieve pressure and reduce Stress. Even if your task is usually challenging, the activities here are made to help you relax and minimize stress.

Screw it up off - Since deep breathing shows up naturally, yoga breathing is frequently overlooked, yet it's a great stress reducer. Breathe while tucking inside your tummy and feel the environment as it grows your lung area as well as your upper body. Breathe towards the count number of four and keep this for just two minutes, and then breathe out to the count number of 4.

Take 2 to 4 deep breathes many times per day, and quickly daily causes may be "eliminated with all the blowing wind!"

Get right up and extend - Imagine the stress water damage from your back, legs, shoulder blades, and put away of your convenience and feet. Increase your stretches by firmly taking enough time to understand a few yoga exercise positions, which you can find in books and videos and also yoga exercises classes.

Take a brief walk after lunchtime or instead of an espresso break - A fast ten or fifteen-minute walk every day isn't just literally beneficial, yet exchanges your concentrate from the problems towards the landscapes along your path, whether it is the good-looking person in the hall or the trees and shrubs in a nearby park.

Press a lemon. P. To. Barnum stated, "When lifestyle hands you a "lemon," make lemonade!" Blending a citrus or rugby ball is an excellent way to keep the fingernails from gnawing at into the hands! If you smash the fruits or the golf ball, possibly get a plastic ball or continue to a far more strenuous exercise to lessen your Stress!

Progressive rest is particularly helpful when Stress keeps you from obtaining a good night sleep – Ensure that from your feet to your head experience rest. The best feeling at that moment should be calmness all through the body; foot, ankles, leg muscles, legs, thighs, etc. Up your upper body to your shoulder blades, and lastly to the very best of your mind or on the other hand down throughout your hands to your disposal (if you make it all that much before you're asleep!)

Dance - Sign up for an exercise course, a *Tai chihuahua* course, or start the music and dance. Dance has a two times advantage for reasons along with exercise. Music is a superb Stress reducer.

Chapter 10

What Makes Children Anxious Today?

Consider all the causes that can trigger anxiousness in an average adult's day: Sound, digital activation from Televisions, computers, mobile phones, and additional continuous information-emitting devices, Targeted traffic, Juggling function responsibilities, actions, and family members. For kids, who tend to be vulnerable to sound and uproar, day-to-day Stress trigger could be amplified, producing the necessity intended for silent downtime even more critical. Increase that college and after-school actions, the pressure to achieve success (whether it originates from outside or from within themselves), family adjustments or issues, and a bunch of elements that can result in anxiety in addition to the perfect formula for kid stress.

Indicators of Stress in Kids

Often, kids, especially more youthful children, cannot

completely state their emotions of anxiety and stress. The signals of stress in children might be quite delicate, such as seeing that abdomen aches and pains, headaches, or changes in behaviour. You may even notice disposition swings and sleep issues along with difficulty focusing at school.

If there were any main changes within a child's existence like a move or a fresh sibling, parents should spend particular interest to check out feasible indicators of years as a child Stress. Even though you can not pinpoint a specific stress element, your son or daughter might experience anxiety from something at school or various other resources you aren't aware of.

Keep an eye on her behaviour and moods, watching for any signals of problems. Inquire her instructor about how she is actually doing in school and observe her, if she is actually getting together with relatives and buddies members.

It is also worth it, speaking with your son or daughter in what she might be feeling, although she might not have the ability to state it in "grown-up" conditions. Adhere to queries in what the girl might worry about or factors that may not be making her feel great. Generally, youngsters usually do not grasp the idea of this kind words of as anxiety and stress.

What Parents Can Carry out About Kid Stress

Make your kids know they have access to speak to you - Encourage your son or daughter to talk to you regarding any complications he might be having, and also to discuss his feelings freely and truthfully. Among the most crucial and effective ways, humans can offer with Stress is simply by speaking with somebody about their particular problem.

Even if your son or daughter struggles to communicate what she is annoyed about, particularly merely having you ask and motivating her to chat can change lives.

Make sure you pay attention to your son or daughter before offering recommendations - Just as much as you might like to jump in and help provide solutions, allow her to exhibit her thoughts and feelings before making comments, or expressing your opinions.

Consider doing a task while you chat - Some kids may experience convenience discussing their issues while engaging in a task with a mother or father. Take action both of you enjoy, this kind of, like taking a walk, making cookies, or playing a circular of a golf ball in the driveway just before requesting your kid to go over a problem he might be having.

Research shows that males, specifically, are convenient for posting their emotions if they're involved in exercise while speaking.

Get children to do a few yoga breathing exercises - Encourage your son or daughter to breathe "good" airflow and breathe out "bad" atmosphere, and picture it transporting any concerns out of her body.

Do some yoga exercise poses with your children - Basic yoga exercises position such as downward dog, cobra, and tree are great for kids. Even though you do that for just a short while, each day before college or at night just before bed making, a little peace with you may make a significant difference in a child's day.

Try some quick stress-relief suggestions for kids - These types range from fun activities you can enjoy with each other such while snuggling as well as a book, massage therapy, or playing a preferred game.

How to handle Anxiety in Children

It is an unfortunate yet very actual fact that anxiety and stress in children is undoubtedly a universal problem in the current fast-paced, high-tech, activity-packed society. If your son or daughter is experiencing anxiety and stress, try these types of simple yet effective methods to help her manage her fear, getting worried, and annoyed.

- *Don't Write off Her Emotions* - Telling your son or daughter not to be concerned about her worries might only make her feel just like she's performing something amiss only by sense stressed. Let her know it is alright to feel bad about something and motivate her to talk about her feelings and thoughts.

- *Listen* - You understand how significantly comforting it could be merely to have got someone pay attention when something's bothering you. Do a similar thing for your son or daughter. If this individual doesn't feel just like talking, tell him you are there for him. You need to be unaffected by his action and help remind him that you like him and support him.

- Provide Comfort and Distraction - Try to take action she loves, like playing a favorite game or cuddling within your lap and having you read with her, just like you did when she was younger. When the potato chips are straight down, a pleasant 10-year-old will value a good serving of mother or father TLC.

- *Take Him Outdoors* - Exercise can enhance the feeling, thus get him moving. Sometimes if it is merely for a walk around, oxygen and exercise may be precisely what must lift his spirits and present him a fresh perspective about things.

- *Adhere to Routines* - Balance any adjustments by attempting to keep with a lot of her regular program. Make an effort to adhere to her proper bedtime and meals when possible.

Maintain Your Son or Daughter's Health

Make sure he is eating correct and getting plenty of rest. Not really getting enough rest or eating healthy foods in regular periods can contribute to your child's stress. If he feels good, he'll be better outfitted to sort out whatever is usually bothering him.

- *Avoid Overscheduling*

Soccer, martial arts, football, music lessons, and another set of extracurricular actions kids may take on are endless. Way too many activities can result in anxiety and stress in children. Just like grownups require some outages after work and on week-ends, children likewise need some peace only to decompress.

- *Limit Contact with Distressing News*

If your son or daughter views or listens to upsetting

pictures or accounts of organic disasters, this kind of as earthquakes or tsunamis or views disturbing reports of assault or terrorism on the news headlines, speak to your kid about what's happening. Reassure her that the lady and individuals she enjoys aren't at risk.

Discuss the aide that individuals who are victims of disasters or violence gotten from humanitarian education groups, and discuss techniques she can help with.

- *Consult with a Counselor or Your Doctor*

In the event where there happen to be a modification in the family like a new brother, a move, divorce, or a loss of life of a member of family is at the rear of your son or daughter's anxiety and stress, talk to a specialist such while your son or daughter's college counselor, your paediatrician, or a kid therapist. They can recommend ways to help a kid discuss death, for example, or help him through any other change in the family.

- *Plan a Quiet Example*

You can set the tone about how anxiety and stress in adults

and children are dealt with within your own home. It can practically bring out the question to filter stress from your lives in the current high-tech, 24-hour-news-cycle world; nevertheless, you can take action about how exactly you handle your Stress.

Switch it off, play some soothing music, and try some comforting yoga postures and additional stress-relieving strategies. The higher it is possible to keep stuff calm and peaceful at home, the unlikely it is that stress and anxiety in kids is an issue in your home.

Chapter 11

Preventing Vacation Anxiety and Stress in Children.

The holiday season is a great and memorable time; nevertheless, also an extremely busy one, and vacation anxiety and stress in children may happen. Through the vacations, several fun activities and events are happening, both in homes and school.

Even though that may be an essential thing, the truth is that the state of being hectic means activities tend to be so hot, bedtimes obtain pushed back, and routines are interrupted. Because of this, kids might inevitably feel some extent of vacation stress.

Establish a Quiet Example

The primary way parents can help relieve anxiety in children through the holidays can be by wanting to keep elements relaxed whenever you can. Much like a lot of situations, how parents manage a concern may set the tone meant for how their children will act. In a situation whereby you allow holiday Stress get to you, your children will certainly detect it all, and kid anxiety is certainly much more likely to be always a problem in your own home.

To reduce nervousness in kids through the vacations, do something to take care of your anxiety and stress.

- *Setup Conditions once and for all Behavior*

Prevent taking your son or daughter to locations like the shopping mall or vacation gatherings when he's starving or exhausted. It's hard to even for grown-up to cope with noise and a lot of activation when they're not sensing their most exceptional; kids get hungry more regularly and exhausted quickly, and could understandably possess trouble, getting on the most significant behaviour and will encounter holiday Stress when they are exhausted or hungry.

- *Keep in mind the Need for Routines*

The holiday season can toss a huge wrench tool into home routines, which can likely make the kinds involved in stress. To reduce vacation stress in your children, make an effort to get habits back on the right track once a meeting or party has ended. For example, if a college vacation concert or a chapel gathering will go before your child goes to bed, make an effort to adhere quietly to informal activities the very next day and get your son or daughter to bed promptly another night time.

- *Watch What They May Be Consuming*

Avoid all the excess sugary vacation snack foods and having less time for you to sit back to regular foods, it could be possible for babies to consume much less well-balanced meals, which could donate to vacation anxiety and stress in children. Try packaging healthful snacks, when you have to shop for the vacation, ensure that you reduce the amount of reasonably sweet treats at home. Whenever you can offer healthful snacks, this kind as of air-popped popcorn or apple pieces with cheese products and crackers and limit cookies and candy to after-snack goodies.

- *Get Your Son or Daughter Moving*

Oxygen and workout are crucial to enhance mood and resetting the spirit, which could alleviate vacation anxiety and stress in children. Be sure you routine a while to get your kid outside to walk around and play.

- *Prevent Overscheduling*

The attractiveness of the vacation might convey the presence of relatives and buddies, make an effort to limit your vacation celebrations and activities so that you and your kids don't get too confused as to the large population turn up. Several occasions, weekly, might be beautiful, yet having a responsibility each day can result in vacation anxiety and stress in children.

Grown-up like to help dad and mom, mainly if they will get plenty of commendation to be accountable and helpful. When you have to shop, inquire your son or daughter to assist you in looking for something at the shop (fun stocking stuffers just for cousins, for example). Providing your child with a job can not only increase her self-pride; it'll distract her and assist in preventing any holiday anxiety and stress.

- *Schedule A Few And Quiet Peace*

Having some tranquillity with your son or daughter is more essential than ever before throughout the occupied Christmas season. Look for a silent part and read a publication with your son or daughter or create vacation pictures intended for grandpa and grandma. Go for a walk outside in character, far from sound and crowds and responsibilities. Help remind your son or daughter and yourself what the holiday season is actually about.

An excellent antidote to getting vacation Stress and the puffed-up commercialism of the growing season is usually supporting others, whether it is by shoveling a senior neighbor's pavement or by merely wrapping presents for clingy kids in your neighborhood chapel. Helping your grade-schooler turn into a charitable kid can help relieve her vacation anxiety and stress.

Chapter 12

Handling Anxiety and Stress in Kids

Signs of anxiety and stress in kids often arrive as physical or behavioral changes. Kids react in a different way to Stress depending on the age, specific personalities, and coping abilities, which can trigger many parents to forget the underlying conditions that may be leading to their infant's behavior.

Parents need to identify the indications of kids Stress and also to search for the possible causes. Parents can generally help kids manage anxiety and stress; however, many kids may come with panic and may reap the benefits of a specialist.

Signs of Stress in Kids

Children might not recognize their panic and stressful problems. This may result in a variety of physical and behavioral symptoms to emerge, and parents might be uncertain whether the symptoms are anxious or a medical condition.

Some typically common indications of anxiety and stress consist of:

- Behavioral or Emotional changes.

- Problems concentrating

Behavioral changes - this kind is moodiness, aggression, a short temper, or clinginess.

Signs s to watch out for are;

- He or she is pulling out from family members or close friends.

- She is refusing to go the school.

- They are engaging in trouble in school.

- Hoarding components of appearing insignificance.

Physical

- Reduced or increased hunger.

- Complaints of tummy pains, or headaches.

- Bedwetting.

- Sleep issues, or disturbing dreams.

Other physical symptoms

It can benefit you to take into account whether these signals typically happen before or after particular activities and whether you will find physical symptoms, such as pain, fevers, allergy, or diarrhoea that could transmit a medical problem.

Common Factors behind Child Years Stress

The foundation of stress in kids can be something external, like a problem in school, modifications in our family, or discord with a pal. Anxious emotions may also be the effect of a child's inner feelings and stress. Some typically common factors behind anxiety in children consist of:

- *Significant Modifications in Family*

Main life adjustments that can result particularly in children include divorce, a death in the family members, moving, or maybe the birth of a fresh sibling. These types of seismic changes can rock and roll your child's world. Main life adjustments can quiver your child's sense of security, resulting in confusion and stress and anxiety. For instance, "a fresh cousin can make a kid feel vulnerable and envious." "A loss of life in the family can easily create security alarm that could induce worries on the subject of loss of life and death."

- *Parent Instability*

Cash and work concerns, family members turmoil, and parental disappointment can result in a strong sense of powerlessness about children who may believe that they would like to help but don't possess the methods to do so.

- *Overly-Packed Schedules*

Continuously running in one activity to some others can result in a lot of Stress for kids who generally need several quiet downtimes occasionally.

- *Academic Pressure*

Many kids experience nervousness about attempting to prosper at school. Academics pressure is standard in kids who fear so much about making errors or who have a fear of not being proficient at something.

- *Recognition*

For young grade-schoolers, this anxiety may be considered a common problem. Because they grow older, the majority of children need to squeeze into kids of high esteem and become like them, as well as the pressure to squeeze in and become well-known can be distressing. Cliques and the sensation to be excluded generally become a concern once children enter quality school.

Bullying is usually a significant issue for most kids. It could be refined, or apparent, and could result in physical damage.

Children who also are bullied often feel ashamed regarding being targeted, plus they might conceal the bullying from parents or instructors meant for concern with sketching focus on their particular recognized weak points.

Catastrophic Event on the news headlines

Information headlines and pictures teaching organic disasters, terrorism, and assault can be distressing for kids. When babies see and hear about awful news occasions, they could get worried that something terrible may eventually happen to someone they like.

A Frightening Movie or a Book

Imaginary stories may also cause problems or stress in kids. Children are generally suffering from chilling, violent, or upsetting moments from a show or pathways in reserve. Some children might become more delicate to press content material than others, and it's brilliant to know very well what may annoy your son or daughter, to limit violent mass media content, and adhere to age-appropriate films, books, video gaming, and other press.

How to Help Your Son or Daughter

You will find out that your son or daughter often react to Stress in a very healthy way; they only require some help and assistance. You can assist using the methods listed below:

At Home

- Help your house be a calm, safe, and sound spot to arrive.

- Produce a relaxed house atmosphere and invest in a program. Family member's meals or game evenings can prevent panic and help reduce stress.

- Monitor your son or daughter's TV shows, video gaming, and books.

Make them involved

- Provide your son or daughter with advance notice on any anticipated adjustments that should happen soon. For instance, if you'll be going for a new job in a new town, what this will mean to them is that they are moving into a new school, new close friends, and a new home.

- Involve your son or daughter in social and athletics, exactly where they can easily be successful.

- Enable opportunities, exactly where your son or daughter may have control of a predicament in your daily course.

Your activities

- Adopt healthful behaviors, the kind that helps to

- control your Stress in healthy ways. Kids often imitate their parents' actions.

- Offer affection and encouragement.

- Make use of positive encouragement and ways of self-discipline that promote healthy self-esteem.

- Figure out how to pay attention to your kids without having to be critical or solving complications on their behalf.

- Offer assistance to show your son or daughter methods to comprehend and solve the issues that annoyed them.

- Look out for new signals and actions of conflicting stress.

Look for the guidance of the healthcare practitioner, counselor, or therapist if the signals of stress tend not to reduce or if your son or daughter becomes more withdrawn, stressed out, or even more unsatisfied. Problems in college or when getting together with friends or family is also one more cause designed for concern.

Panic can be an all-too-common problem confronted by kids today. Concerning a child's anxiousness, youthful grade-schoolers might not have the ability to grasp or describe their own particular emotions.

Older children might be able to understand what's disturbing them, although that's simply no assurance that they'll talk about that information with mother or father. Being conscious of adjustments in your son or daughter's behavior will undoubtedly enable you to capture complications before they further affect your son or daughter.

Chapter 13

Stress Management Ideas

People who figure out how to deal with stress and business live a happier, healthier life; below, here are some tips to assure you retain Stress away.

- Maintain the right attitude.

- Accept that we now have occasions that you can not control.

- End up being assertive rather than aggressive.

- Claim your emotions, opinions, or values rather than becoming furious, defensive, or unaggressive.

- Find out and practice relaxation methods; try yoga, yoga exercise, or tai-chi just for stress administration.

- Exercise frequently. The body may battle Stress better when it's fit.

- Consume healthy, well-balanced food.

- Figure out how to manage your time and effort more effectively.

- Set limits correctly and figure out how to say zero to demands that could produce extreme Stress in your daily life.

- Make time for interests, passions, and relaxation.

- Obtain enough rest. The body requires time to recuperate from nerve-racking occasions.

- Avoid relying on alcoholic beverages, drugs, or compulsive behaviors to lessen stress and anxiety.

- Seek out friendly support. Spend plenty of time with those you love.

- Seek treatment with a psychiatrist or various other mental doctors been trained in Stress management or biofeedback ways to learn healthful means of coping with the stress in your daily life.

Breathing Approaches for Stress Relief

- Take a breath in, right now, allow it out. You might notice a notable difference in how you are feeling already. Your breathing is usually a robust device to help ease Stress and cause you to feel much less stressed. Several simple respiration exercises could make a significant difference if you make sure they are part of your regular.

Before you begin, maintain these pointers at heart:

- ✓ Choose a spot to do your inhaling and exhaling physical exercise. Maybe it's inside your bed, in your living space floor, or an appropriate chair. This may cause you to feel more pressured. Put on comfortable clothing and try to get it done at the same time a few times a day.
- ✓ Engage in many deep breathing exercises, which takes just a few moments. When you have additional time, you can do all of them for ten minutes or even more to get sustained benefits.

- ✓ Meditation: A lot of people consider short, superficial breaths to their chest. It could cause you to experience stress and zap your energy. With this system, you will understand how to consider bigger breaths, entirely into the stomach.
- ✓ Get comfort. You can lie on your back bed or on to the floor with a cushion under your mind and legs, or you may sit down in a seat with your shoulder blades, head, and throat backed against the trunk of the seat. Breathe throughout your nose.
- ✓ *Allow your tummy filled up with air.*
- ✓ *Inhale away throughout your nose.*
- ✓ *Place one hand on your stomach.*
- ✓ *Place the additional hands in your upper body.*
- ✓ *As you breathe, feel your belly rise.*
- ✓ *As you inhale out, feel your tummy reduce.*
- ✓ *The hands-on your stomach should exercise than the main one that's on your own upper body.*

Breathing Focus

When you do yoga breathing, use an image in your thoughts and a term or term to help make sure you are feeling calmer.

- ✓ *Close your eye if they're open up.*
- ✓ *Have a couple of big, deep breaths.*
- ✓ *Breathe. As you do this, suppose the environment is usually filled up with a feeling of peacefulness and relaxation. Make an effort to feel it during your body.*
- ✓ *Breathe in out. As long as you're doing it, suppose the environment leaves with your Stress and stress.*
- ✓ *Now make use of a phrase or expression along with your breathing.*
- ✓ *As you breathe, say in your thoughts, "I breathe peace and relax.*
- ✓ *As you breathe out, say in your thoughts, "I exhale out Stress and pressure."*
- ✓ *Continue for 10 to twenty minutes.*
- ✓ *Equivalent Time intended for Sucking in and Deep breathing out*

With this workout, you'll match how prolonged you breathe in with just how long you breathe out. As time passes, likely to increase just how long you can inhale-exhale at the same time.

- ✓ *Sit comfortably on to the floor or in a seat.*
- ✓ *Breathe through your nose; seeing that you need to do this, count number one to five.*
- ✓ *Gently breathe out through your nose towards the count of five.*
- ✓ *Replicate many times.*

Once you are feeling more comfortable with breaths that last five minutes, boost how lengthy you breathe and inhale and exhale out. You could work up to breaths that last up to 10 minutes.

Intensifying Muscle Mass Relaxation

In this system, as you breathe in, you make a muscle mass group anxious and breathe out as you release this. Intensifying muscle mass relaxation can help you relax bodily and psychologically.

- ✓ *Lie comfortably on to the floor.*
- ✓ *Have a few deep breaths to unwind.*

- ✓ *Breathe; tenses the muscles of the feet.*
- ✓ *Take in the air away. Launch the stress within your foot.*
- ✓ *Breathe. Tense your leg muscles.*
- ✓ *Exhale out. Discharge the stress inside your calves.*

This helps to make the parts of the body function properly; your hip and legs, stomach, upper body, fingers, hands, shoulders, and throat.

Modified Lion's Breath

- ✓ *While you do this exercise, suppose you're a lion. Allow yourself to breathe out immensely, open up mouth.*
- ✓ *Sit down comfortably on to the floor or within a seat.*
- ✓ *Breathe through your nasal area. Fill up your belly entirely up with your surroundings.*
- ✓ *Open the mouth area as large as possible. Inhale and exhale out with an "Ahh."*
- ✓ *Do it again many times.*

Techniques for coping with Stress determine the causes in your daily life. As easy as it seems, many people are not conscious enough to what gives them anxiety, nor will everyone get the same nerve-racking. One individual's stress could be another's problem or inspiration.

Likewise, few people realize just how much their very own thoughts, emotions, and manners contribute to their particular stress. All of us are responsible for how exactly we interpret occasions in our lives. We are accountable for habits such as procrastination, unfinished business, and inattention towards our businesses that leads to deadline concerns, not spending expenses promptly, and failure to perform essential jobs which usually, subsequently, trigger stress.

Consequently, the first critical stage is to recognize the causes of stress and Stress in your daily life and the methods you are using to work on them.

- *Simplify your daily life* - If you're burning up yourself out by doing a lot of exercises, start reducing on a few of your unsuccessful, yet frustrating and energy-draining actions. No-one can perform everything.

Establish your focal points and make space for carrying

out what you worth and discover most significantly.

Similarly, it is essential to understand how to say NO! Delegate and redistribute duties when you have to, yet don't make an effort to do everything. Hire a cleaning support, one day weekly, get an infant sitter to get the youngsters after school, have got a yard service the actual landscaping design.

Feeling pressured and overburdened originates from dealing with an excessive amount of rather than managing it with rest and down-time.

Five Methods For A Sensible Existence

- **Decrease Effects of Stress by consuming well, working out frequently, and getting enough sleep** – Many at times when we are starving or exhausted, we are extremely pressured and grumpy. Not getting the nutrition your body needs causes both mental and physical stress; therefore will not obtaining enough rest.

    Regular physical exercises do not just produce

anxiety and Stress as long as you're carrying it out; it creates endurance and endurance, helping you to deal with pressure better. A lot of people take too lightly the need to keep excellent physical wellness to defend against anxiety and stress.

Great things about Routine workouts

- *Acknowledge that there is a specific situation we cannot modify* - As everybody knows, there are a lot of things in life that are beyond control, like the loss of life of someone you care about, job reduction, disease, etc.

As hard as it could be at first, in such instances, an essential thing we can do is acknowledge the fact that these things are beyond modification. Secondly, we can choose to respond to the function in several constructive methods, which include:

- Expressing whatever you're going through to a pal or therapist (recovery).

- Keeping a diary to record thoughts and emotions (cathartic).

- Searching for possibilities for development; and learning from it (active).

- Developing strength (building internal resistance).

There are more prevalent factors behind unavoidable Stress, such as job selection interviews, taking an exam, needing to make a presentation, a disagreement with someone, and similar circumstances.

In such instances, it can help to learn how to remain as made up as you possibly can. Yoga breathing techniques, creation (emotionally rehearsing the function), and planning yourself as much beforehand, dramatically, reduce the stress you can experience.

Manage Stress in healthful ways

Are you dealing with stress with a suitable method or harmful method? If you are dealing with anxiety using a delicate process, you are compounding the problem.

> Cruel ways of managing stress consist of; **abusing alcoholic beverages, taking numerous pills, cigarette smoking, over or under consumption, viewing excessive TV**, Stress management strategies helps to take away your worries, and generally avoid problems.
>
> If you're already stressed, but you are still working out your stress using harmful techniques, you make issues much worse only by compounding the stress.

Not surprisingly, most of us have exclusive response to stress and how exactly we select to take care of this. The secret is usually to discover what works for you. Study shows that stress reducer is how much you can rest physically and mentally. *Harvard's Herbert Benson, Meters. D. The technique wonders that it merely needs no particular position or place.* For example, in the event whereby you will be trapped in visitors, or if you are having trouble drifting off to sleep; here's just how:

- ✓ Sit back comfortably. Close your eye and loosen up muscle tissue.
- ✓ Breathe in deeply, to make sure that you are inhaling and exhaling deeply, place one particular hand in your belly, the other on your own upper body.
- ✓ Inhale gradually throughout your nasal area so that as you are doing so, you should feel your abdomen (not your upper body) rise.
- ✓ Gradually exhale, concentrate on your inhaling and exhaling.
- ✓ If thoughts start to interfere, avoid dwelling on all of them, permit them to fade away, and to concentrate on your breathing completely.
- ✓ You can decide to switch to working out if you feel stressed. Carrying it out regularly for about 10 to 20 minutes a day can place you within a generally

relaxed mindset, which could get you through typically stressful circumstances.

Much Healthier Methods to Control Stress:

- Meditation, yoga exercises, or biofeedback techniques are kinds of mind influx therapy.

- Exercise simply by taking a walk, weight lifting, jogging,

- Spend some time outside at sea, in a bad neighborhood, or cruising,

- Make an appointment with a buddy,

- Have a hot, aromatic bath,

- Get a massage,

- Pay attention to calming music,

- Reserve twenty minutes per day to do whatever you desire,

- Watch a comedy film or display - this relieves pressure.

Harmful ways to cope with stress:

- Extreme drinking.

- Using drugs or pills to unwind.

- Sleeping a lot off.

- Viewing television for a long time.

- Pulling out from interpersonal activities.

- Obtaining your stress from others.

Dangerous Effects of ongoing Stress:

- Negatively changes the body and human brain chemistry (stress hormones, cortisol).

- Weakens your disease fighting capability.

- Cardiovascular disease, hyperStress, coronary attack, stroke.

- Depressive disorder of stress and anxiety.

- Ulcers, stomach irritabilities.

- Pores and skin problems, hair thinning.

- Headaches, migraine headaches.

- Sexual disorder.

Everybody knows that life could be stressful, occasionally it's preventable and sometimes not; nevertheless, if we consider strictly how exactly we deal with stress and put into action using effective ways, pressure can be a functional element of everyday routine.